WRITED BY

Millie Lorelle Magee

All rights reserved

Welcome to the exciting world of space and the solar system! In this book, we will explore the amazing things that exist beyond our planet Earth.

The solar system is a group of planets, stars, moons, asteroids, and comets that orbit around the sun. The sun is a star that gives us light and warmth. The solar system has eight planets: Mercury, Venus, Earth, Mars, Jupiter, Saturn, Uranus, and Neptune. Each planet is unique and different from the others.

There are also many moons that orbit around these planets. Some planets have no moons, while others have many. These moons are also unique and fascinating in their own way.

We will also talk about the amazing things that humans have done in space, like landing on the moon and sending telescopes like the Hubble and Webb to explore the universe.

Are you ready to explore space with us? Let's blast off and discover the wonders of the solar system!

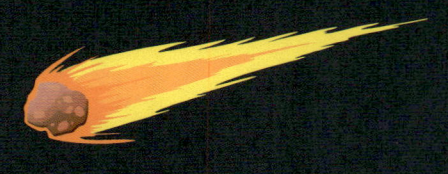

Meet your crew!

Panda Lily - deputy commander of a space expedition.
She is very brave and clever, and very friendly to her crewmates. She loves to speak to children and teach them about space.

Pig Amelia - Pilot of the spacecraft.
She is very skillful and courageous, and very competent in her work. She is always ready for the adventures and challenges that await her in the space.

Bear Max - Crew mechanic.
He is very skillful and always ready to fix any technical problem that may arise aboard the spacecraft. He likes to discover new things and is very curious.

Tiger Jacson - Space explorer.
He is very intelligent and loves to explore new planets and planetary systems. He is always looking for new ways to increase his knowledge of the cosmos.

Cat Leo - Space navigation specialist.
He is very agile and skillful, making him an ideal space navigation specialist. He always carefully plans the spacecraft's travel routes and makes sure the crew reaches their destination safely.

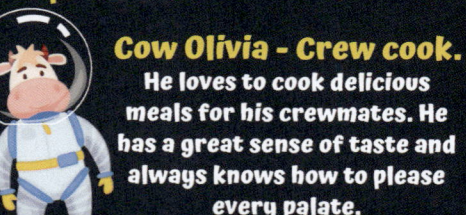

Cow Olivia - Crew cook.
He loves to cook delicious meals for his crewmates. He has a great sense of taste and always knows how to please every palate.

Koala Grace - Crew scientist.
He is very intelligent and is always looking for new ways to increase his knowledge of the cosmos. He is very creative and likes to experiment.

Sloth Ethan - Researcher of extraterrestrial life.
He is very calm and composed, and very inquisitive. He enjoys spending time observing the various life forms he encounters on his way through space.

Rabbit Bolt - Shipboard engineer
He is very skillful and skilful in his work. He is always ready to fix any device aboard the spacecraft.

You - You Are the Commander of the crew.

Photo or Draw →

What is Solar System?

The solar system is like a big family of planets that all live together. The sun is like the daddy of the family because he is the biggest and brightest.
Then we have the planets, which are like the kids in the family.
They are all different and have their own personalities.
Mercury is like the smallest and runs around really fast, while Jupiter is the biggest and loves to play with his many moons.
There are also some other things in the solar system, like comets and asteroids, which are like the cousins that come to visit sometimes.
All of these things are always moving and spinning around, just like how we like to play and move around too!
In our solar system, there are eight planets.
Their names are Mercury, Venus, Earth, Mars, Jupiter, Saturn, Uranus, Neptune and "Dwarf Planet" Pluto. Some are big and some are small, some are hot and some are cold, and some have rings around them! All of these planets move around the sun in their own special orbit, just like how a bike goes around a track.

When we go to space, we need to wear a special suit called a spacesuit. This is because space is very different from Earth - it's very cold and has no air to breathe! The spacesuit is like a big, protective bubble that keeps astronauts safe.
The spacesuit has a helmet that covers their head, just like a bike helmet. This is to protect their head from any bumps or debris that might be flying around in space.
The spacesuit also has a special material called a "combinezon" that covers their body. This material helps to keep the astronauts warm and protects them from harmful radiation that comes from the sun.
So, wearing a combinezon and helmet is really important for people who go to space, because it helps to keep them safe and healthy while they explore the cosmos.

Sun

Mercury

Moon

Venus

Earth

Jupiter

Mars

Uranus

Saturn

Neptune

Pluto

5

Sun

The sun is a Star is like a big, bright light bulb in the sky. It's like the daddy of the planets because it's the biggest and most important. It gives us light and warmth, just like how a blanket keeps us cozy. The sun is always shining and never takes a break, but sometimes it likes to play games with us by hiding behind the clouds. Without the sun, we wouldn't have daytime or be able to grow plants and food. We should always remember to be grateful for the sun and how it takes care of us.

- The sun is super hot, much hotter than anything we have on Earth. It's like a giant oven! The temperature on the sun's surface is about 5,500 degrees Celsius (9,932 degrees Fahrenheit).
- Even though the sun looks like it's moving across the sky, it's actually us who are moving around the sun. The Earth spins on its axis once a day, and it takes one year for the Earth to orbit around the sun.
- The sun is really, really big. In fact, it's so big that you could fit over one million Earths inside it!
- The sun is a big ball of gas, mostly made up of hydrogen and helium. It's so huge that its gravity is what keeps all the planets in our solar system orbiting around it.
- The sun is also really fast. It's hurtling through space at about 220 kilometers per second (137 miles per second) - that's like driving a car from New York to Los Angeles in just one minute!

Mercury

8

Mercury

Mercury is a planet that's really, really hot (800 degrees Fahrenheit (430 degrees Celsius), But at night, the temperature on Mercury gets really, really cold - as cold as -290 degrees Fahrenheit (-180 degrees Celsius)!! It's the closest planet to the sun, and the sun shines really bright on it all the time. Mercury is smaller than Earth, but it's still bigger than a lot of other things in space. It doesn't have any air to breathe like Earth does, so nobody can live there. It's covered in rocks and dust, and it's always really quiet because there's no wind to blow things around. Mercury is a cool planet to look at, but we can't visit it because it's too hot and too far away.

Because Mercury is so close to the sun, it's very hard to study. Only two spacecraft have ever visited Mercury - Mariner 10 in the 1970s and the Messenger spacecraft in the 2000s. Scientists are still learning new things about this small, rocky planet!

Venus

Venus

Venus is the second planet from the sun and is sometimes called Earth's "sister planet" because they are similar in size and structure. However, Venus is a very different planet in many ways.

Venus has a thick atmosphere made mostly of carbon dioxide gas. This atmosphere traps heat and makes Venus the hottest planet in our solar system, with surface temperatures that can reach up to 465 degrees Celsius (869 degrees Fahrenheit) - hot enough to melt lead!

Venus also has very long days - one day on Venus (the time it takes to complete one rotation) is longer than one year on Venus (the time it takes to complete one orbit around the sun)! This means that Venus spins very slowly, taking about 243 Earth days to rotate once on its axis.

Because of its thick atmosphere, Venus is covered in clouds that make it hard to see its surface from space. However, scientists have used radar to map the surface of Venus and have found volcanoes, mountains, and valleys on this interesting planet.

Even though Venus is similar in size and structure to Earth, it's a very different place with extreme temperatures and a hostile environment.

Earth

12

Earth

Earth is where we live! It's a big round ball that's covered in land and water. It's special because it has air that we can breathe and that keeps us safe from the sun. Earth is home to lots of different animals and plants, like birds, trees, and flowers. We have day and night because Earth spins around like a top, and it takes one whole day for it to spin all the way around.

But did you know that we have a friend that travels with us in space? It's our Moon! The Moon is a big, gray rock that floats around Earth. We can see the Moon at night, and sometimes during the day too! The Moon is really far away, but it looks close because it's so big! It takes one whole month for the Moon to go around Earth. Sometimes the Moon looks round and bright, and sometimes it looks like a little slice. We must be kind to our Earth and our Moon so that they can keep being happy friends for a long, long time

Mars

Mars

Mars is a planet that's sometimes called the "Red Planet" because it looks red in the sky. It's a lot like Earth in some ways, but also very different! Mars is very cold and dry, and there's no air to breathe. It's not a place where people could live.

One of the coolest things about Mars is that it has the biggest volcano in the solar system! It's called Olympus Mons, and it's three times taller than Mount Everest, the tallest mountain on Earth! Mars also has the longest canyon in the solar system, called Valles Marineris. It's so big that if it were on Earth, it would stretch all the way from New York to Los Angeles!

Mars also has two small moons named Phobos and Deimos. They are very different from Earth's moon because they are irregularly shaped and look like potatoes! Scientists are still trying to learn more about these moons and how they formed.

Another interesting fact about Mars is that it has seasons, just like Earth does! This is because Mars also spins around a big star called the Sun. However, because Mars is farther away from the Sun than Earth is, it takes longer for Mars to go around the Sun. This means that its seasons last longer too!

Even though Mars is very different from Earth, scientists are still very interested in studying it. They send rovers and spacecraft to Mars to learn more about its environment and whether or not life could exist there in the future. Who knows, maybe one day people will even be able to visit Mars and see its amazing landscapes up close!

Jupiter

16

☄️ Jupiter ☄️

Jupiter is the big brother of the planets because he is the biggest and loves to play with his many moons! He is very big and has lots of colorful stripes on his surface.

The environment on Jupiter is very windy and stormy. A giant storm on Jupiter called the Great Red Spot has been raging for hundreds of years!

The temperature on Jupiter is very cold, even though it is the biggest planet. This is because he is very far away from the sun.

Jupiter has lots of moons - more than any other planet! The four biggest moons are called Io, Europa, Ganymede, and Callisto. They are very interesting because they are covered in ice and some even have volcanoes!

Isn't Jupiter so cool and interesting?

Jupiter is also known for having a very strong magnetic field, even stronger than Earth's. This means that Jupiter has very powerful auroras, just like Earth, but they are much bigger and brighter!

Jupiter is so big that you could fit all of the other planets in the solar system inside of it! But don't worry, Jupiter is too far away from us to ever cause any harm.

Jupiter is also very important because it helps protect Earth from dangerous asteroids and comets. Its strong gravity pulls these objects toward itself instead of toward Earth, which keeps us safe.

I hope you found these fun facts about Jupiter interesting!

Saturn

Saturn

Saturn is the sixth planet from the Sun and is about 886 million miles (1.4 billion kilometers) away from it. It's also the second largest planet in our solar system and is about 95 times more massive than Earth!

Saturn is another big planet, just like Jupiter, but it has something that makes it extra special - its beautiful rings! Saturn's rings are made up of tiny bits of ice and rock, and they look like a big, shiny belt around the planet.

Saturn is also known for having lots of moons - over 80 of them! One of its moons, called Titan, is especially interesting because it has an atmosphere just like Earth, and even has lakes and rivers made of liquid methane instead of water.

Even though Saturn is really far away from the Sun, it still gets very hot because of all the gas that makes up its atmosphere. But don't worry, no one lives on Saturn - it's just a big, beautiful planet for us to look at from far away.

Another interesting fact about Saturn is that it has very strong winds, with some gusts reaching speeds of up to 1,100 miles (1,800 kilometers) per hour! That's faster than the fastest airplane in the world!

Overall, Saturn is a fascinating planet with many unique characteristics that make it stand out from the rest of the planets in our solar system.

Uranus

Uranus

Uranus is another planet in our solar system, and it's a very special one! It's named after the Greek god of the sky, and it's the seventh planet from the sun.

Uranus is a very cold planet, with temperatures that can get as low as -370 degrees Fahrenheit (-223 degrees Celsius) ! That's even colder than your freezer at home. It's also a very windy planet, with winds that can blow up to 560 miles per hour.
That's faster than a race car!

One of the most interesting things about Uranus is that it spins on its side! This means that instead of spinning like a top, it rolls around the sun like a ball. It takes Uranus about 84 Earth years to make one trip around the sun, and a day on Uranus is about 17 Earth hours long.

Uranus also has 27 known moons, and they're all named after characters from William Shakespeare's plays. Isn't that cool? Some of the moons are named after characters like Miranda, Ariel, and Titania.

Uranus is a very unique planet, and there's still a lot to learn about it. Maybe one day, humans will be able to visit Uranus and explore its icy world and its many moons!

Neptune

Neptune

Neptune is a big blue planet in our solar system. It's very cold there because it's so far away from the sun. The temperature on Neptune is about -200 degrees Celsius or -392 degrees Fahrenheit! That's much colder than your freezer at home. Neptune is surrounded by very strong winds, much stronger than any winds on Earth. The winds can blow up to 2,100 kilometers per hour or 1,300 miles per hour! That's faster than a race car!

Neptune has 14 moons! Some of them have really interesting names, like Triton, Nereid, and Proteus. Triton is the biggest moon of Neptune and it's very cold there too, even colder than Neptune itself.

Scientists think that Neptune might have a big ocean under its thick layer of gas. And who knows, maybe there are some interesting creatures living in that ocean!

Pluto

Pluto

Pluto used to be known as the ninth planet in our solar system, but now we call it a dwarf planet. It's very far away and very cold, much colder than our freezers at home!

Pluto doesn't have much air, so if you went there, you would need to wear a special suit to breathe. And because it's so cold, everything on Pluto is frozen solid.

Pluto also has a few little moons that orbit around it. They are called Nix, Hydra, Kerberos, and Styx. They are very small, but they are still important members of Pluto's family.

Did you know that Pluto was named after the Roman god of the underworld? That's because it's so dark and far away, just like the underworld in ancient myths.

Pluto is a very interesting and mysterious little world, and scientists are always learning new things about it.

Moon

Moon

The moon is a big, round rock in the sky that we can see at night. It looks like a big circle, but sometimes it looks like a banana or a smiley face!

The moon is always changing shape, and we call these changes "phases". Sometimes it's a big, bright circle and sometimes it's just a little sliver.

The moon is also very important because it helps us have tides in the ocean. The tides are like the ocean's big breaths, and they go in and out because of the moon's gravity pulling on the water.

Some people even think that one day we might be able to visit the moon and walk on its surface, just like we walk on the ground!

Milky Way

Do you ever look up at the sky and see all the twinkling stars? Well, did you know that all those stars together make something called a galaxy? And guess what, we live in one of those galaxies called the Milky Way! The Milky Way is really big and has millions and millions of stars, just like our sun. And it's not just stars, there are also planets, moons, asteroids, and comets, all swirling around together in this big galaxy.
It's amazing to think that we live in a galaxy that's so big and full of so many amazing things. And who knows what else we might discover as we keep exploring and learning more about the Milky Way!

Constellation

A constellation is a group of stars that people imagine make a picture in the night sky. Just like how you might imagine a cloud looks like a bunny or a dragon, people imagine stars in the sky to look like animals or things too! There are many different constellations, and they have special names like Orion or the Big Dipper. When you look up at the stars at night, see if you can find any constellations in the sky! Let me show you couple of them on next pages.

Orion:

This is one of the most recognizable constellations and is named after the mythological hunter Orion. It contains some of the brightest stars in the sky, including Betelgeuse and Rigel.

Ursa Major

Also known as the Big Dipper, this is one of the most well-known constellations and is visible throughout the year in the northern hemisphere. It is named after a bear and is easy to spot because of its distinct shape.

Cassiopeia

This constellation is named after a queen from Greek mythology and is visible in the northern hemisphere. It is known for its distinctive "W" shape.

Aries

This constellation is named after a queen from Greek mythology and is visible in the northern hemisphere. It is known for its distinctive "W" shape.

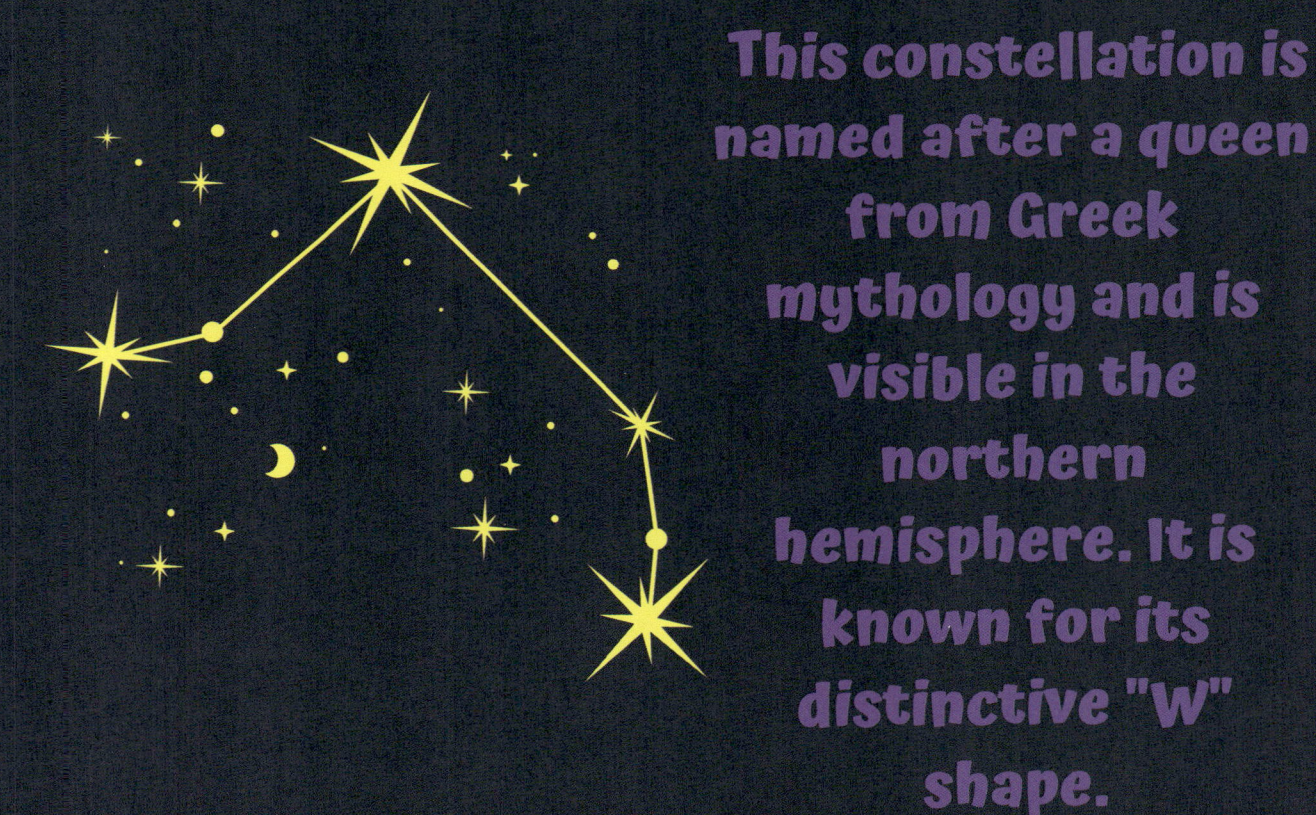

33

Taurus

Taurus looks like a big, strong bull with pointy horns. People born under this sign are said to be very determined and hardworking.

Gemini

Gemini looks like two stars next to each other, and they are twins! People born under this sign are said to be very friendly and good at communicating with others.

Cancer

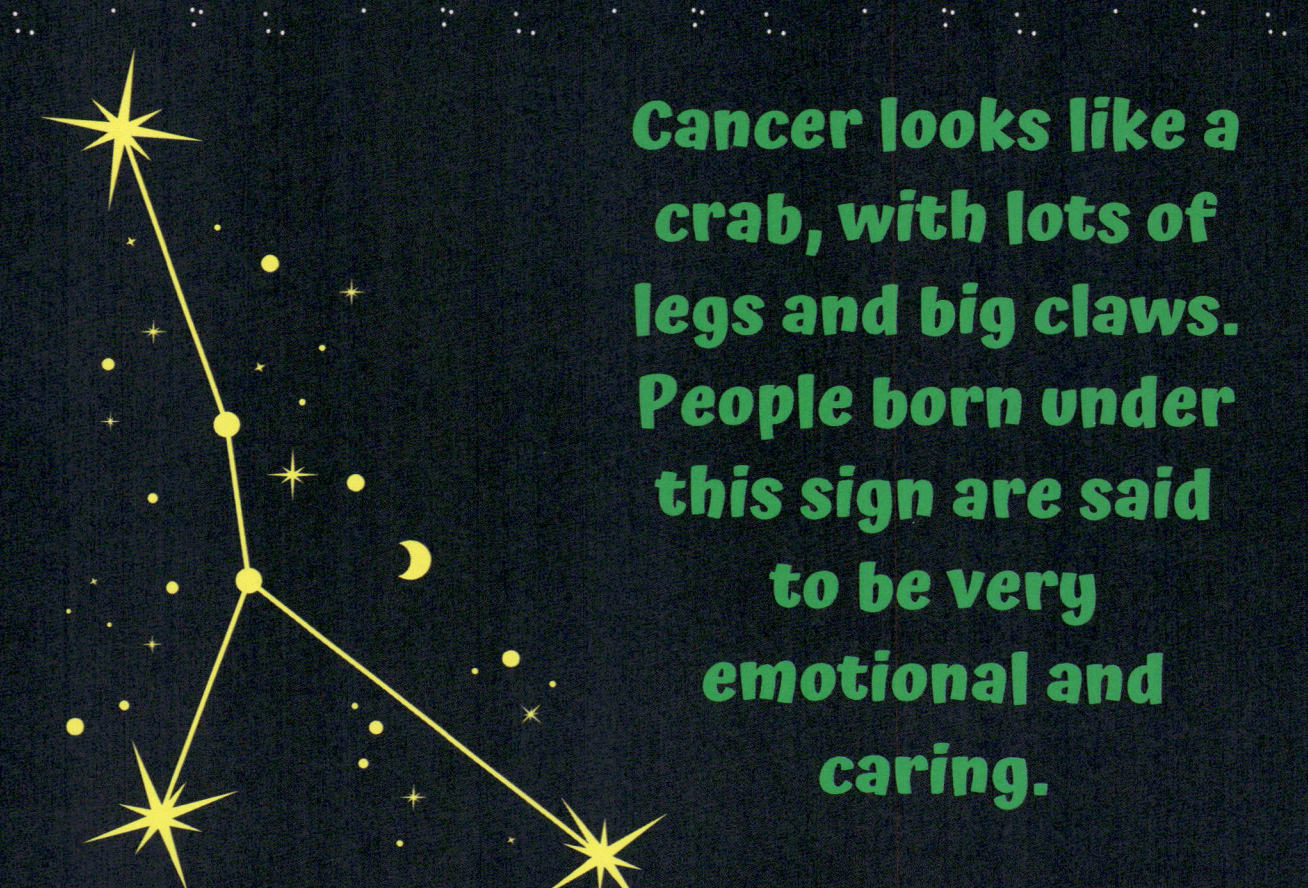

Cancer looks like a crab, with lots of legs and big claws. People born under this sign are said to be very emotional and caring.

Leo

Leo looks like a lion, with a big mane and sharp claws. People born under this sign are said to be very confident and strong.

Virgo

Virgo looks like a woman holding a sheaf of wheat. People born under this sign are said to be very detail-oriented and organized.

Libra

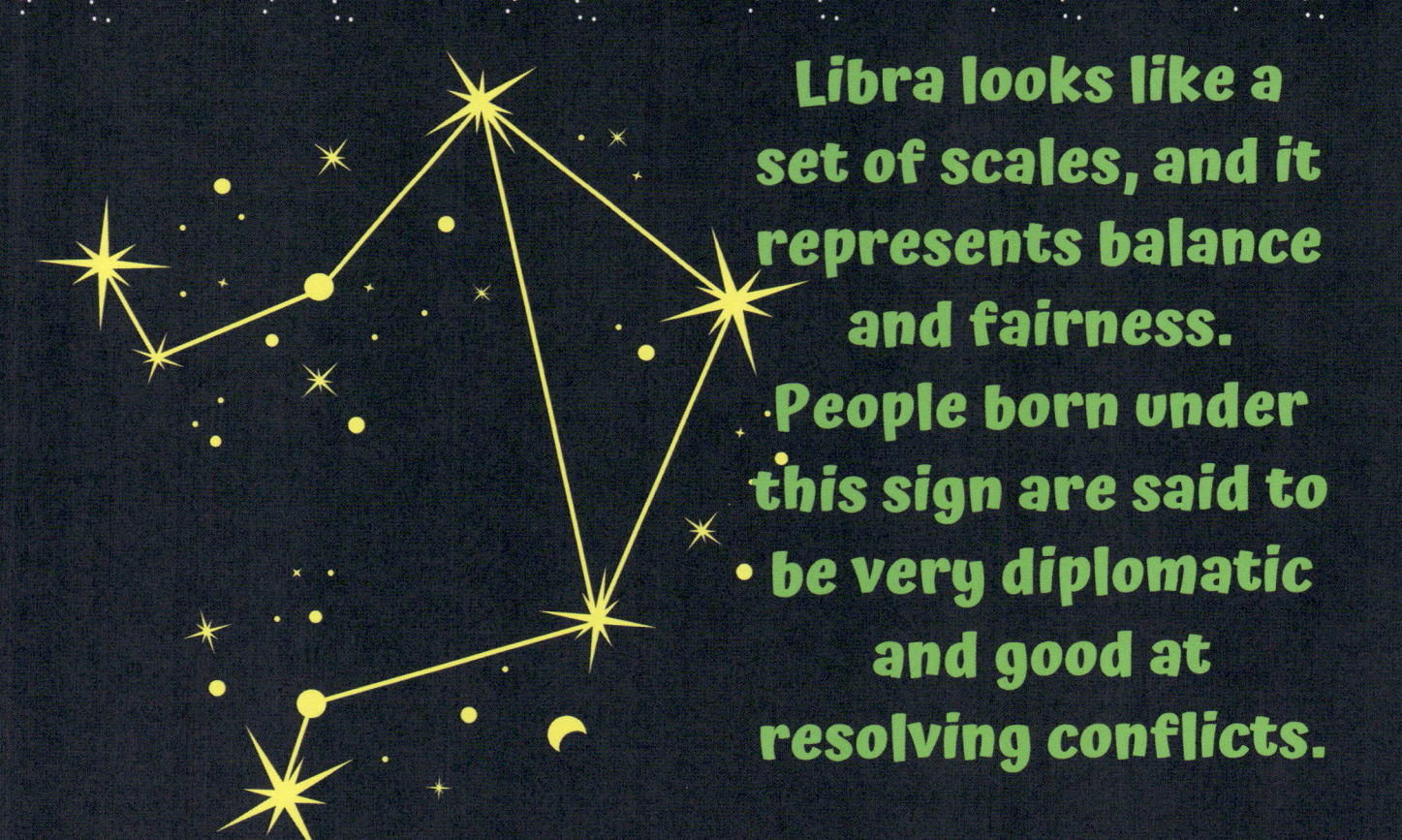

Libra looks like a set of scales, and it represents balance and fairness. People born under this sign are said to be very diplomatic and good at resolving conflicts.

Scorpio

Scorpio looks like a scorpion, with a stinger tail and big pincers. People born under this sign are said to be very intense and passionate.

Sagittarius

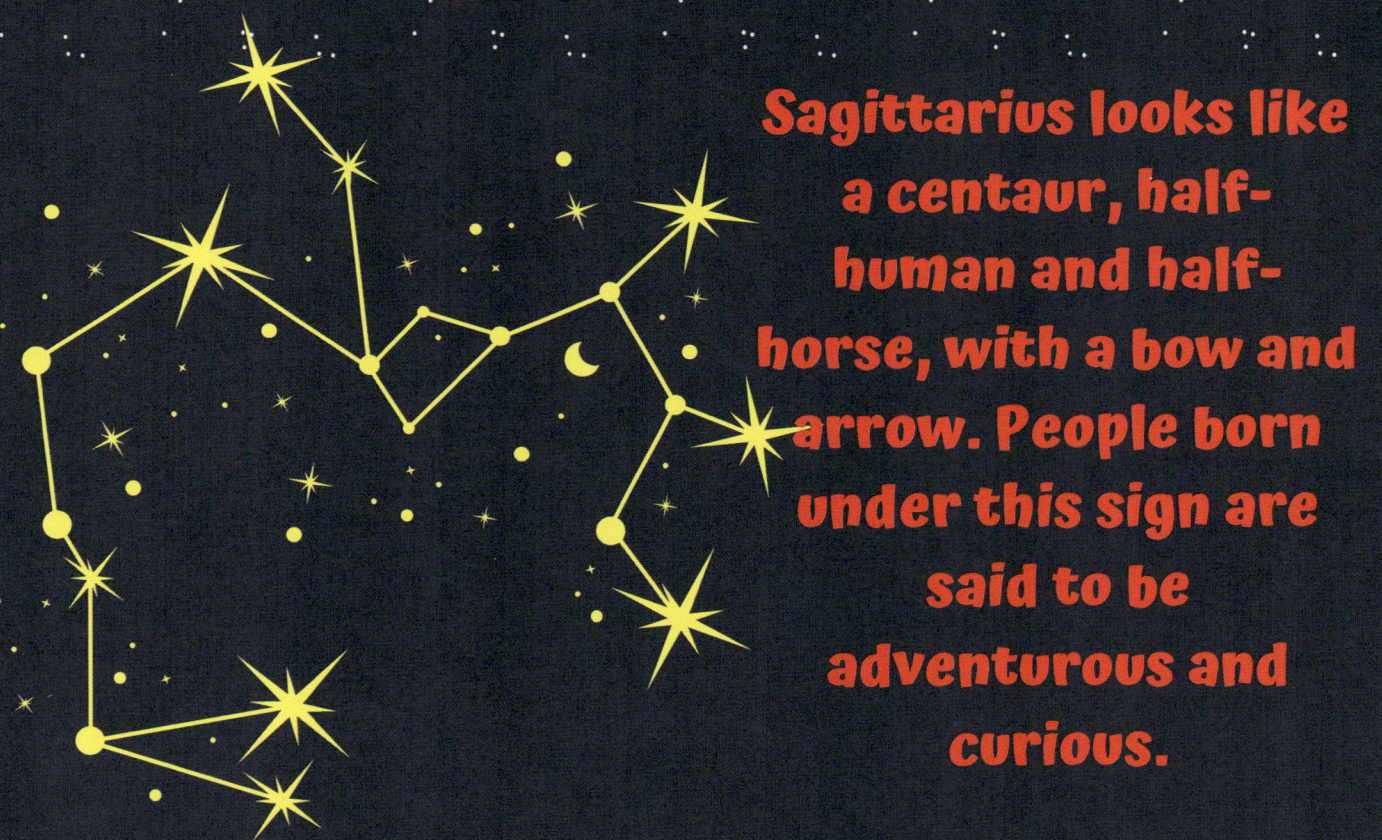

Sagittarius looks like a centaur, half-human and half-horse, with a bow and arrow. People born under this sign are said to be adventurous and curious.

Capricorn

Capricorn looks like a goat with a fish tail. People born under this sign are said to be very ambitious and hardworking.

Aquarius

Aquarius looks like a person pouring water out of a jar. People born under this sign are said to be very independent and creative.

Aquarius

Aquarius looks like a person pouring water out of a jar. People born under this sign are said to be very independent and creative.

Pisces

Pisces looks like two fish swimming in opposite directions. People born under this sign are said to be very intuitive and compassionate.

Did You Know ?

A long time ago, in the year 1969, some brave astronauts (Neil Armstrong and Edwin "Buzz" Aldrin) went on a super cool mission to land on the moon! They flew a spaceship called Apollo 11 all the way from Earth to the moon. When they got there, they wore big, puffy suits that looked like superheroes and walked on the moon's surface. They even left a flag there to show that humans had been there! They collected rocks and did some experiments to learn more about the moon. Then they came back home to Earth as heroes! It was a really big deal and people still talk about it today.

Did You Know ?

In the year 2020, a special spaceship was launched from Earth with a very important mission. It was headed to Mars, a planet that's very far away from us! The spaceship was called "Perseverance" and it was very big, almost as big as a car.

Perseverance had lots of special tools and equipment to help it explore Mars. It even had a special robot arm with a drill to take samples of the Mars rocks and soil! And there was a special helicopter onboard too, called "Ingenuity", to fly around and explore Mars from the air.

After traveling through space for many months, Perseverance finally landed safely on Mars in February 2021. It was a very exciting moment for all the scientists and engineers who worked on the mission!

Perseverance has been exploring Mars ever since, sending back lots of pictures and information about the planet. It's helping us learn more about Mars and maybe even find clues about whether there might be life there in the future!

Did You Know ?

The ISS, or International Space Station, is like a big house that floats in space! Astronauts from all around the world live there and work together to learn about space and how to live in space.

The ISS is really big - as big as a football field! It has lots of rooms and even a gym for the astronauts to exercise in. They also have a cool room with big windows where they can look at Earth and see how beautiful our planet is.

The astronauts on the ISS do all sorts of important jobs. They do experiments to learn about space and how to live there. They also help fix things that break and make sure the ISS is always working properly. Sometimes, astronauts go outside of the ISS to do work, too! They wear special suits to keep them safe while they're outside, and they get to float around in space. How cool is that?

The ISS is always moving really fast - so fast that it goes around the Earth 16 times every day! That means the astronauts get to see a sunrise and a sunset every 45 minutes. It must be so amazing to see the Earth from up there!

Did You Know ?

The Hubble Space Telescope is a big, special telescope that orbits around the Earth. It was named after a famous scientist named Edwin Hubble. The telescope is very important because it can take pictures of things in space that are very far away, like stars, galaxies, and planets.

The Hubble was launched into space in 1990 by a special spaceship called the Space Shuttle. It had a little bit of trouble at first because the pictures it took were blurry, but then astronauts fixed it and now it can take really clear pictures!

Scientists use the pictures from the Hubble to learn more about space and how it works. They have discovered many amazing things with the Hubble, like new galaxies and planets that are very far away. The Hubble has helped us learn a lot about space and our universe.

Did You Know ?

The Webb Telescope is a big space telescope that floats in space like a giant eye. It's named after a man called James Webb who wanted to see faraway things in space more clearly. The Webb Telescope can see things that are really, really far away and hard to see with regular telescopes on Earth. It has a big mirror that's much bigger than a car and it can collect lots of light from faraway stars and galaxies. This helps scientists study space in more detail and learn about how things in space work.

The Webb Telescope was built by lots of people who worked really hard to make it. It took a long time to build, almost 20 years, and cost a lot of money.

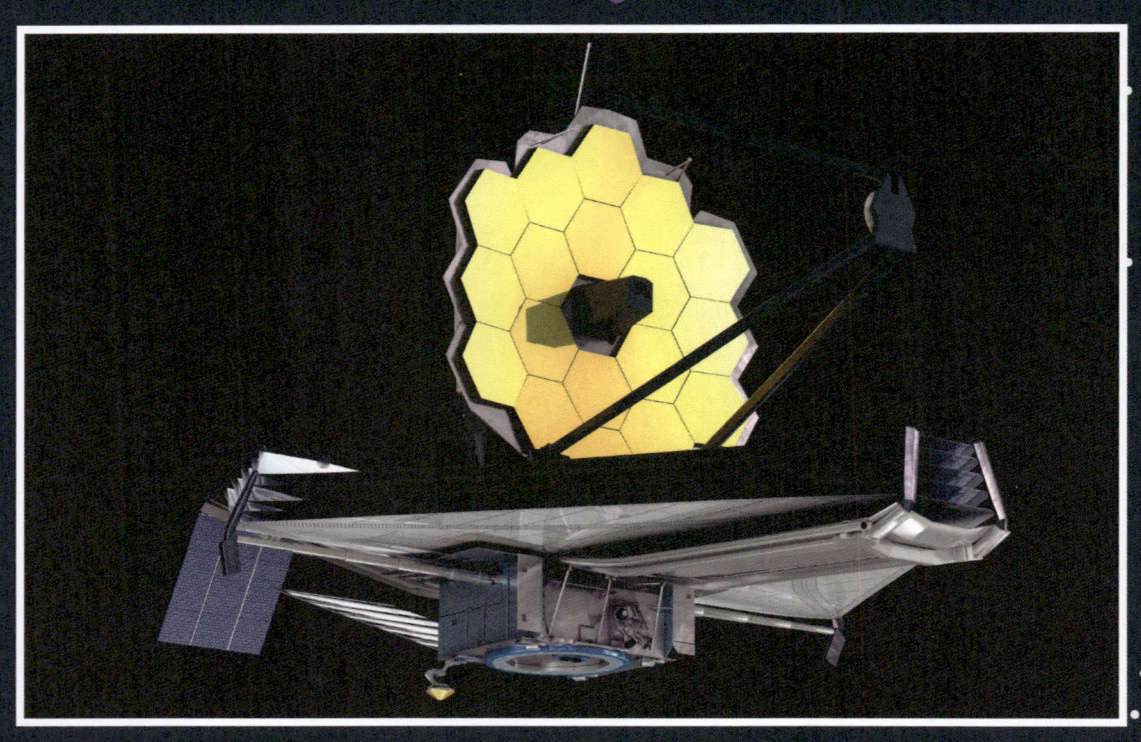

Did You Know?

An asteroid is a big rock that floats around in space. Sometimes, asteroids come close to Earth, but don't worry, they usually don't come too close. Scientists study asteroids to learn more about the solar system and where we all came from. Some asteroids are very small, but others can be as big as a whole city!

Did You Know ?

A comet is like a big, dirty snowball that flies through space. It has a head that is made of ice, dust, and rocks, and a long tail that shines when it gets close to the sun. When a comet comes near the sun, the heat makes some of the ice and dust turn into gas, and the gas streams out behind the comet to make its tail. Comets come from very far away, and they can take many years to make a complete journey around the sun.

Did You Know ?

Black holes are like big vacuums in space. They're places where gravity is so strong that nothing can escape, not even light. When a really big star runs out of fuel, it can collapse in on itself and become a black hole. Black holes are invisible because they don't let any light out, but we can see their effects on other things around them, like stars that are getting sucked in. Black holes are really strange and mysterious, and scientists are still learning more about them every day.

Did You Know?
Quick Facts!

- One day on Venus is longer than one year on Venus.
- The coldest known place in the universe is the Boomerang Nebula, which is -457.6°F (-272°C).
- If you could drive your car to the moon at a steady speed of 60 mph (97 km/h), it would take about six months to get there.
- Astronauts in space grow taller because their spines elongate without gravity compressing them.
- The universe is estimated to be around 13.8 billion years old.
- If you could travel at the speed of light, you could go around the Earth 7.5 times in just one second!
- The Great Red Spot on Jupiter is a massive storm that has been raging for at least 350 years!
- Scientists estimate that there may be up to 100 billion planets in our Milky Way galaxy alone.
- The Milky Way, which is our home galaxy, contains billions of stars and is about 100,000 light years across. That means it would take 100,000 years to travel from one end of the Milky Way to the other at the speed of light!

Hope You Enjoy

Table of contents

- **Welcome** — 2
- **Meet Your Crew** — 3
- **Solar system and planets** — 4-27
- **Milky Way** — 28
- **Constellations** — 29-45
- **Interesting Facts** — 46-54

Printed in Great Britain
by Amazon